WORKBOOK

For

A Practical Guide to Dr. Gabrielle Lyon's Book

Forever Strong

A Guide to A New, Science-Based Strategy for Aging Well

By

H. KolithPress

Copyright©2023 by H. KolithPress

All Rights Reserved

This book and any part of it should not be copied, transmitted, stored, exhibited publicly, or reproduced in any form or manner without the express permission of the author and/or publisher.

Why you need this workbook

This workbook provides a concise and high-level summary on a chapter basis of the best-selling book "Forever Strong" by Dr. Gabrielle Lyon. The workbook aims to illuminate and simplify all the concepts highlighted in the main book.

Healthy living is essential for a happy and fulfilled life. The alternative can be depressing, expensive, painful, and as such totally undesirable. The key to a healthy life is not far-fetched but there are no shortcuts.

This book recommends practical and scientifically proven steps, techniques, actions, and consciousness to guide you toward a healthy, long, and fulfilling life void of illness and diseases. It also challenges old beliefs and misconceptions with proven theories backed by sound research.

Grab your copy and begin to take your initial steps to a healthy life.

Introduction

The aim of the book is to help the reader understand the practical steps of healthy living and how to actualize a realistic healthy body regardless of the person's current body weight. It helps reconfigure the mind to focus on the right things and tools necessary for good health. The book aims to help the reader find freedom from being overweight or obese by implementing workable practices and still being able to maintain a healthy nutritional diet. It unveils that the key to a healthy body isn't necessarily a weight problem but rather a muscle problem and uses this book to express the discoveries on this subject matter.

The goal being to achieve extraordinary health, the **Lyon Protocol** focuses on promoting muscle health as its driving force by combining nutritional instructions and training instructions with operating procedures which will yield the power to make real lasting improvements to one's body composition and overall health.

Having a mindset reset is very effective. This unveils that there are drivers of behaviors categorized into two; *the fixed mindset and the growth mindset*. Understanding that there are drivers of this behavior is essentially needed to have effective results in health, seeing that there is a fixed mindset and a growth mindset. Also understanding which a person possesses will greatly help in channeling appropriate results. It emphasizes that the mindset required is the growth mindset as pairing it with internal discipline is crucial, as it integrates a growth-focused mental framework.

Part One
THE STAKES

CHAPTER 1

Shift the Fat-Focused Paradigm

Objectives

- This chapter aims to discuss the importance of addressing daily lifestyle factors such as diet, exercise, etc.

- Studying and reviewing the various factors including societal and physiological that make it challenging for individuals to make lasting changes to both health and fitness.

Summary

The chapter begins with the story of the doctor's patient, a forty-six-year-old chef who suffered from rheumatoid arthritis which left her fatigued and in pain, her name was Layla and she weighed 317 pounds at the initial time. Pointing out that Layla wasn't alone in the struggle and that obesity is widely prevalent in the United States, and although a good number of persons are informed in some basics of what to do to avoid this reality like the need to eat better and exercise often, they still find it difficult to implement the change.

Furthermore, several people are trapped in nothing of feeling exhausted, overwhelmed, and lured into false ideas about their own ability to change, which has in the long run prevented them from making the very changes that build a foundation for long-term health and longevity, but in this chapter, the author shows a way to get out of this loop.

For Layla the first thing was to get her moving by simply incorporating three additional ten minutes of walks throughout the day, after that, she began with resistance exercises to assist with quality weight loss helping to decrease fat tissue without sacrificing muscle, and of course, her nutrition was the next thing that was put in check, the focus was to anchor her first and last meal with protein while eliminating snacking, and seven months, Layla lost nearly sixty pounds, and losing this weight wasn't the only benefit as her initial joint pain decreased and her blood markers also improved and at the end, Layla felt less hungry, more encouraged and much better.

Focusing on mainly fat and not on skeletal muscle, which is the internal muscle that drives all systems, sends people down the wrong path. The muscle, which is a dynamic tissue and makes up about forty percent (40%) of a person's mass, does far more essential work than improving appearance or athleticism, as is the keystone organ of health. Therefore, the first step in changing your body inside out is repairing damaged muscles and building new lean muscle mass.

The healthier muscle an individual has, the greater the ability of the body to maintain homeostasis/balance, and the major key is training your mind to also become an asset rather than a liability.

Critical lessons from the chapter

- Obesity is a common issue in the United States, and more than 70% of people are overweight.

- Lifestyle factors such as poor diet, lack of exercise, smoking, and sleep quality can highly contribute to the risk of heart disease, stroke, and type 2 diabetes.

- Implementing lifestyle changes can greatly reduce the risk of these bad health conditions.

- A lot of factors, which include psychological, physiological, societal, and religious factors, can make it challenging to adopt healthier habits.

- It's important to break free from the mindset of relying on quick fixes and instead focus on sustainable changes for better health and well-being.

Exercises drawn from the chapter

- What lifestyle factor does the CDC estimate help in resolving most of the heart disease, stroke, and type 2 diabetes cases?

- To what percentage does addressing lifestyle factors reduce the risk of these chronic diseases?

- What are some factors that can make it harder for us to get into shape?

_____
_____
_____
_____
_____
_____
_____
_____

- What name is the life-fortifying tissue also called?

_____
_____
_____
_____

- How is well-timed resistance training beneficial?

_____
_____
_____

- What are the five ways to make muscle magic?

- What is the first muscle you need to work on?

CHAPTER 2

Thwart Disease

Objectives

- It aims to move the focus of modern medicine towards muscle as the fountain of youth.
- To Empower individuals to take control of their health by improving muscle mass.
- To also help repair your metabolism and muscle tissue, even if it's infiltrated with fat.

Summary

This chapter begins with positive remarks and positions the reader to have a mindfulness of being able to repair both his metabolism and muscle tissue even if he has had unfavorable results in the past. It emphasizes that if one would use and focus on "The Lyon Protocol" one will not only be able to improve the health status of the current existing muscle but also to build more.

Also, studies have shown that it is important to build muscles to protect you as you age and this is done if only one focuses on supporting a muscle-centric perspective on longevity, because losing muscle quality can be equated to losing the metabolic advantages of muscle, specifically power, strength, and mitochondria and these disadvantages are not necessarily subject to age.

Furthermore, it is expected that as a person gets older, the body's breakdown of muscle (catabolism) proceeds at an accelerated rate and if it's left unchecked the body could attain a positioning of constant decline. This is why it is vital to build muscle (anabolism), thereby readjusting the balance and protecting oneself from catabolism for a very long time.

Lastly, the chapter emphasizes that it isn't too late to make the diet and exercise changes that can melt away muscle marbling and get one back on track and this can easily be carried out by following the Lyon Protocol. It has been noted that building muscle mass before disease strikes offers our best defense against conditions such as Cachexia, and even after diagnosis, targeted nutrition and exercise programs that promote and maintain skeletal muscle provide immediate interventions that can boost Cachexia survival rates and even help recovery.

Critical lessons from the chapter

- You can repair your metabolism and muscle tissue, even if it's infiltrated with fat.

- Most times, the Western medical system usually overlooks the importance of muscle in preventing illness.
- Muscle is the real fountain of youth and can greatly improve health outcomes if taken care of.
- Increasing healthy muscle mass can provide greater protection against mortality and morbidity.
- It is of great importance to connect immediate symptoms to long-term health repercussions.
- Muscle mass should be considered an important biomarker for overall health.

Exercises drawn from the chapter

- What is sarcopenia?

_____
_____
_____
_____
_____
_____
_____
_____

- Which does more damage losing muscle or gaining fat?

_____
_____
_____
_____
_____
_____
_____
_____
_____
_____

- What do you lose when losing muscle quality?

_____
_____
_____
_____
_____
_____
_____
_____

- How can the process of aging be slowed?

___

- What is the fountain of youth?

___

- What is the three-part formula for making changes?

___

CHAPTER 3

Bulletproof Your Changing Body for Strength at Every Age

Objectives

- To help Establish a healthy system of viewing aging and prioritize the quality of life.
- To learn how to decode your body's changes and understand the reasons behind implementing strategies.
- To help you know the importance of muscle health in maintaining mobility.

Summary

This chapter begins by gearing the reader into the undeniable reality of daily aging and that it's a reality that is unavoidable, but then the reality of the outcome is dependent on the choices made basically from one's wealth of knowledge which can either give one a quality aging experience, and a major determinant of one's life quality is the muscle being that it is essential for mobility.

Also, emphasis is made on starting earlier and younger as it is equally vital for young people to build and maintain healthy muscle tissue as this act will lay the proper foundation for longevity, and just as it is in banking early investment in muscle health reaps reward that compound over time. Even amongst children, there are benefits of muscular fitness characterized by strength, power, and local muscular endurance. Exercise is also beneficial to cardiovascular health in young people, and strength training in kids also increases their capacity for motor neuron recruitment, offering them a lifelong benefit.

Muscle tissue is much more responsive at the early stage and this is basically because young people exist in a hormone-driven growth phase, so if strength training is performed safely at developmentally appropriate levels it would naturally lay the groundwork that would last a lifetime, although the book isn't geared towards kids the **Lyon Protocol** actually lays out sound principles for eating and exercise that can benefit the whole family.

The healthier your muscle mass, the greater your chances of living and thriving, so it is essential that one begins to build up and start immediately and not postpone till a later date because the truth will remain that quick fixes never work but instead following a step by step model will be more profitable and in this case following the Lyon Protocol will establish a solid foundation upon which to build a future of strength, good health and longevity.

It is mentioned that fertility is tightly linked to diet and lifestyle in both men and women and that obesity is known to disrupt female fertility and being slightly overweight can be associated with decreased pregnancy rates, while for men, fat causes a decrease in testosterone by converting it to estrogen and in the long run decreases men's fertility but on the other hand muscle contraction may positively affect reproduction, the catch being if fat is folding up fertility, growing healthy muscle which will improve metabolism can help unfold.

Critical lessons from the chapter

- Aging is a natural process that affects everyone, but our choices can impact on our quality of life.

- Plan for the natural changes that come alongside aging and commit to nutritional and training strategies.

- Disease states can be gradual and addressing them before they become severe is possible.

- Strategies can be implemented to prevent and counter declines in physical health.

- It is never too late to start taking care of the body and improving your well-being.

- Priority should be on the quality of life, focusing on maintaining muscle health for mobility

Exercises drawn from the chapter

- What is the benefit of resistance exercise and nutrient-rich foods for young people?

_____
_____
_____
_____
_____
_____
_____
_____

- At what age do the inevitable physiological changes to muscle and overall body composition start?

_____
_____
_____

- What attributes determine older people's ability to maintain strength and muscle mass?

- What age will one likely reach peak bone mass?

- What is the best defense for a pregnant woman's baby as mentioned in this chapter?

- What is the term used when men experience testosterone decrease?

- How are you to engage future projections?

Part Two
CHART YOUR ROAD MAP TO SUCCESS

CHAPTER 4

Slam-Dunk Success with Nutritional Science

Objectives

- To learn about the history and science of nutrition to correct any misconceptions.
- To find accurate and reliable nutritional information to create a good lasting plan.
- Developing critical thinking skills so that we can make informed daily choices and evaluate new health information.

Summary

The chapter begins with addressing a major obstacle faced when the person is on the part of becoming healthier which is knowing the right nutritional guidelines, and the solution proffered was simply by examining clinically verified publicly available data which will help avoid confusion on the subject. The author proposed the Lyon protocol's nutritional strategies as a safe bet to a successful outcome.

The author emphasizes that knowing what to do isn't just sufficient but also knowing how to think is equally vital in the aspects of nutrition to bring a discerning eye to one's daily choices and vet any new health information that comes along the way. The objective of this is to show how science reflects the perspective of each historical moment in the space of nutrition to help the reader have a base on food science information.

The first notion was that nutritional recommendations have been influenced by political and policy considerations from the very beginning instead of optimal health for individuals. Religion and religious leaders have played a vital role in their choices. Over the years government-funded nutritional guidelines have never helped individuals achieve exceptional health to prevent deficiencies

Focusing on an area of food science e.g. Fat at the expense of another e.g. protein can leave us with skewed information, but then this focus on one area has left protein undisputed for ages and helped maintain its importance, recently once a patient's overall energy need is determined the first and most important nutrient to calculate into their diet is protein and after which the remaining calories including carbohydrates and fat is added, but although this is the required/recommended training dietitians receive the current government's guidelines first addresses carbohydrates and fats before allocating protein recommendations, as a percentage of energy in relation to the other macronutrients.

We are expected to also set standards and not just goals in our routine, and this can greatly be learned from elite military operators who normally abide by a set of principles, just as Viktor Frankl put it, "pain is inevitable, but suffering is optional", this is because we can train our minds and get rid of harmful mental clutters and this will benefit not just the mind but also the body as a whole.

Critical lessons from the chapter

- Dietary guidelines have always been influenced by political and policy considerations throughout history.

- There are a few external factors such as politics, social agendas, morality, and religion which also shaped and influenced nutritional science.

- Sylvester Graham, a Presbyterian minister, played a significant role in promoting vegetarianism.

- Graham believed that a simpler, plainer, and more natural diet could combat social, spiritual, and physical corruption and he also influenced nutrition science.

- When the historical context of dietary guidelines is understood, it can help unravel the complexities of nutrition science.

- Individual health and optimal nutrition were not always the primary focus of dietary recommendations.

Exercises drawn from the chapter

- What are the two keystones of nutrition that can help bring a discerning eye to daily choices as stated in this chapter?

- Who is referred to as the father of vegetarianism?

- What kind of diet did Sylvester Graham call for?

- What is the problem of nutritional science?

- What is the kind of evidence that should inform your health?

- What are the three hierarchies of evidence?

- Why is dietary advice confusing and often contradictory?

- Are you willing to practice vegetarianism and why?

CHAPTER 5

Protein: More Than Just a Macronutrient

Objectives

- Aims to help in the understanding of the diverse functions of proteins in the body beyond just the physical structures.
- To show the importance of proteins in supporting the immune system and its mediators.
- To make known the significance of dietary protein for longevity, metabolic function, and quality of life.

Summary

This chapter begins by giving the essentials of protein in the body and how it does not just compose twenty percent (20%) of the body's composition but also a macronutrient that acts as the master regulator of all that is happening in the body, controlling functions in all tissues and organs including muscles. Protein also includes enzymes (a class of proteins that catalyze all the chemical reactions within the body).

As a result of the essential role of protein, it is evident that these functions make protein critical for longevity, metabolic functions, and quality of life, although these new discoveries of dietary protein have evolved greatly the information is still not yet properly disseminated such that even physicians are still sharing outdated recommendations, but this book has given the opportunity to gain clarity on the proper protein consumption that's necessary based on current research.

Since all the tissues in the body are proteins and in a year's cycle nearly every one of them (these proteins) gets replaced, it is essential to ensure that one has sufficient and proper nutrients to meet and exceed these requirements. Also, by eating for muscle health, one will simultaneously meet all the primary biological needs while also optimizing for body composition.

The author stated the fact that the quality of protein will affect the quantity intake, optimal health generally requires that one pays attention to the amino acid composition of different foods, if lower quality protein sources are chosen then they'll need to consume greater quantities of food supplement options. In all, animal protein contains the highest quantities of essential amino acids and will be able to supply the amino's critical for sustaining the body's protein.

Lastly, it is important to have an appropriate meal timing, and when it comes to getting muscles, breakfast is actually the most important meal being the first meal of the day. it should be started with a robust dose of protein, as this will help set up the body for metabolic optimization, priming the body by stimulating muscle growth, reducing hunger, and supplying with an amino acid dose to use for other biological processes, and then, the second most important meal is the last meal before retiring from the day to the bed, choosing foods that provide your body with sufficient amino acids to generate glucose can help stabilize blood sugar throughout the night and prepare for the morning.

Critical lessons from the chapter

- The body is roughly composed of 60% water, and half of the remaining 40% is made up of protein.

- Proteins are not just responsible for physical structures in your body. They also help in the regulation of all the functions happening inside the body.

- Enzymes which are a class of proteins also play a crucial role in catalyzing chemical reactions within your body.

- Protein-rich foods are essential for producing neurotransmitters that aid brain-cell communication.

- Protein is very necessary for longevity, metabolic function, and overall quality of life.

- Although the Scientific understanding of the importance of dietary protein has evolved, there many people who are still uninformed.

- There are still several outdated recommendations about protein intake that persist, even among some physicians.

Exercises drawn from the chapter

- Why shouldn't protein be ignored?

_____
_____
_____
_____
_____
_____
_____
_____
_____
_____
_____
_____

- What are the three different types of amino acids needed to maintain overall health?

___

- How can muscle and tissue breakdown be prevented?

- How many amino acids are designated essential?

- Why does the quality of protein affect the quantity?

- What are complementary proteins?

- What meal is the most important when it comes to making muscles and why?

CHAPTER 6

Carbohydrate And Dietary Fats: Demystifying the Darlings of Nutritional Science

Objectives

- It aims to help Understand the impact of overconsumption of starchy, sugary refined carbs on metabolism, obesity, insulin resistance, and type 2 diabetes.
- To help identify that not all carbs are created equal and that even whole grain-based carbs can contribute to imbalances in body composition.
- To challenge the mainstream thinking about carbs and fat by looking at the "calories in, calories out" and insulin-carbohydrate models.

Summary

Carbohydrates and fats are responsible for obesity in humans, and this is centered around two models which are calories in, calories out, and the insulin-carbohydrate model.

Too much carbohydrate can cause an increased insulin response which in turn increases the amount of storage fat slowing down metabolic rate. There are also two types of carbohydrates mentioned which are fibrous and starchy, the fibrous is made up of long chains of simple sugar molecules that are hard to digest, and the starchy or sugary which are rapidly digested into sugar units.

Glucose is not an essential dietary nutrient because it can be made by the body, and it is needed for fueling the brain, neurons, RBC, kidneys, and pancreas. Carbohydrates need to be consumed for fiber which can be found in fruits and vegetables. The carbohydrate-to-protein ratio defines how many grams of carbohydrate you can have in a meal and still maintain the metabolic balance.

To promote weight loss, the overall dietary carbohydrate-to-protein ratio should be less than 1:0. Food with a carbohydrate-to-fiber ratio of less than 6 has a 10.0 glycemic load and high level of fiber. (A ratio of 8:1 offers a bit more flexibility for those who have the tolerance to carbohydrates hydrates such as whole grains and starches, and vegetables for more nutrient diversity).

Unsaturated fats are predominantly found in plant foods such as vegetable oil, nuts, and seeds. It is helpful for improving blood cholesterol levels and easing inflammation. Sources of monounsaturated fats include olives and avocado, and sources of polyunsaturated fats are walnuts, fish, etc. The essential fatty acids provide the biggest health benefits among the poly-unsaturated fats. Dietary saturated fat becomes a risk only if you are over-consuming calories and carbohydrates. Highly saturated fat concentrations are primarily found in animal-based foods (butter, cheese, and red meat), they can also be found in certain plant-based foods (especially coconut and tropical oils made from coconut, palm, and palm kernels). It is recommended to replace saturated with unsaturated fats, especially poly-unsaturated whenever possible.

Trans fats are manufactured through an industrial process that is used to solidify vegetable oil. It is found in spreads (margarine), baked goods, and fried food (French fries, chicken nuggets, doughnuts, etc.). Trans fats are dangerous because they increase the ratio of heart disease, stroke, and type 2 diabetes, they should be strictly avoided.

Critical lessons from the chapter

- Carbs, can be highly addictive, especially the starchy and sugary ones.

- Overconsumption of processed carbohydrates can lead to obesity, insulin resistance, and type 2 diabetes.

- It is not only packaged and refined foods that could result in nutritional imbalance; even whole grains, fruits, and vegetables count as carbohydrates.

- Whole grain-based carbohydrates which have a low carb-to-fiber ratio can still impact body composition if eaten in excess.

- Carbohydrates can be categorized into fibrous and starchy/sugary types.

Exercises drawn from the chapter

- Which of the two types of carbohydrates is better and why?

_____
_____
_____
_____
_____
_____

- What is the carbohydrate-to-protein ratio and carb-to-fiber ratio?

- Why is poly-unsaturated fat preferred to mono-unsaturated and trans-fat?

- What are the two theories behind the belief that far is bad for health?

- Give some sources of mono and poly unsaturated fats?

- When does dietary saturated fats become a risk?

___

- What are the different types of dietary fats?

___

Part Three

TAKE ACTION: LET LOOSE THE LYON'S ROAR

CHAPTER 7

The Lyon Protocol Meal Plans

Objectives

- It aims to help control hunger by following a protein-forward meal plan.
- To help with the improvement of muscle tone.
- To help in being energized throughout the day.

Summary

The chapter focuses on implementation. It practically helps design a balanced protein-forward diet which is expected to help control hunger, metabolism, and longevity. It is an amazing plan method because one is expected to see results immediately, and some of the benefits of optimizing protein intake include balanced blood sugar, improved muscle tone, supercharged energy, and improved mental clarity.

In addition, the need for consistency is emphasized, and helpful meal-planning techniques are offered, such as creating a regular eating routine and addressing personal shortcomings. Three improvement tracks and an overview were provided to help an individual choose a path based on their objectives to the plans, which center on optimizing longevity, body composition, and muscle mass, respectively. Rotating through each of these three plans will grant access to a legacy of wellness. To calculate calorie demands, the idea of metabolic math highlights the significance of meal journaling based on individual goals, with suggested formulas for fat loss, maintenance, and weight gain. The importance of considering basal metabolic rate (BMR) and total daily energy expenditure (TDEE) is emphasized.

The Lyon Protocol stresses the non-negotiable priority of maintaining steady protein consumption, citing research that suggests protein calories have different effects on body composition compared to carbs or fats, as evidence suggests that dietary protein may be the key macronutrient in terms of promoting positive changes in body composition. The importance of a high-protein breakfast is emphasized, thus, saying one easy strategy to prevent overeating and improve diet quality is prioritizing high-protein foods at breakfast.

The protocol also emphasizes the significance of understanding personal preferences and aligning choices with health goals through an eating-style quiz. The document concludes with a teaser for upcoming details on translating the recommended macro split into actual food choices, emphasizing the importance of discerning between hedonic eating and actual hunger for long-term well-being.

Furthermore, Informed choices regarding carbohydrates are encouraged, with an emphasis on avoiding the consequences of excess carbohydrates that can send blood-glucose levels soaring and drive inflammation and metabolic stress, because of carbohydrate intake at each meal, especially breakfast. So, therefore, prioritizing it with favorable carb-to-fiber ratios is encouraged. Moving on to three health optimization tracks within the protocol: Optimize Longevity, Optimize Quality Weight Loss, and Optimize Muscle, each with specific meal plans and nutritional guidelines set aside to be a goal.

Critical lessons from the chapter

- Living a protein-forward lifestyle can help protect skeletal muscle while fat is being lost.

- The focus of the Lyon Protocol is on intelligent muscle health and arranging intake and output such that it corresponds with health goals.

- Consistent optimization of protein intake will improve muscle tone and support healthy weight loss.

- Lyon Protocol draws attention to the importance of a balanced and protein-rich meal plan for overall health and well-being.

- High-quality protein sources, such as animal-based proteins, provide essential amino acids for optimal muscle-protein synthesis.

- If 30 to 50 grams of protein per meal is consumed it can help maintain skeletal muscle mass.

- Switching to a protein-forward diet can lead to immediate results in reducing cravings and balancing blood sugar levels.

Exercises drawn from the chapter

- What is the BMR and TDEE concept?

_____
_____
_____
_____
_____
_____
_____
_____

- What are the three health-optimization tracks?

- What are the processes in protocol design?

- What are the strategies for meal plan success?

_____
_____
_____
_____
_____
_____
_____
_____
_____
_____
_____

- How many calories does an individual need a day?

_____
_____
_____
_____
_____
_____
_____
_____
_____
_____

CHAPTER 8

Baseline Assessment: Where Are You?

Objectives

- To help Conduct a careful self-assessment to understand your goals and create a plan to reach them.
- To help know how to use numbers from annual physical exams, such as height, weight, waist circumference, blood triglycerides, and fasting blood sugar, to define nutritional needs and goals.

Summary

The chapter begins with the focus of knowing where you are to accurately position for where you want to be and that setting goals is important, and to reach those goals, it's necessary to take a step in assessing where you currently stand. This can be easily done by looking at numbers like height, weight, waist circumference, etc., to get a better understanding of your health risks and what you need to focus on in terms of nutrition. It's also advisable to work with a dietitian and a fitness professional who can guide you, track your progress, and help you make informed decisions about your diet and exercise routine. Having all these metrics can give you a solid starting point.

It can be hard to accurately measure how effective one's workouts are, especially with underlying factors like focus, effort, and self-worth coming into account. But notwithstanding assessing your physical fitness at the beginning of any program is very important, this is because if you don't know where you're starting from, it's hard to know where you're headed.

Although when it comes to food, it's easier to track, evaluate, and measure being that the Doctor can look at a food diary clinically for this evaluation, but when it comes to your training, only you truly know how hard you're working towards your goals. Nevertheless, this chapter helps one to an extent build the structure and support necessary, and by following through one is set to get an environment that will help achieve the extraordinary health one deserves.

It is important to take care of one's heart rate because taking care of the heart and lungs will affect overall quality of life, to measure resting heart rate, you can implement a few options. Some of these are using a fitness watch or a heart-rate monitor, or you can simply use your phone's stopwatch feature and your fingers. The way to manually determine your heart rate in beats per minute (bpm) is:

1. Find your pulse over your radial artery, which is located on the thumb side of your wrist between the bone and the tendon.
2. Count the number of beats you feel in fifteen seconds.
3. Multiply that number by four, and you'll have your heart rate in bpm!

This is a simple way to keep track of the heart rate and make sure you're taking good care of your cardiovascular health.

Critical lessons from the chapter

- Blood pressure readings follow the standards that are set by the American Heart Association and the American College of Cardiology.

- When one engages in an unhealthy diet, physical inactivity, or being overweight/obese, it raises the risk of cardiovascular disease.

- When goals are known, and proper plans created, it makes success easier to achieve in attaining lasting fat-loss changes and maximizing muscle.

- Annual physical exam numbers, like height, weight, waist circumference, etc., can help define your nutritional needs and goals.

- Normal blood pressure is less than 120/80.

- Hypertensive crisis which means very high blood pressure requires immediate medical attention.

Exercises drawn from the chapter

- Why is it important to measure your resting heart rate?

_____
_____
_____
_____
_____
_____
_____
_____
_____
_____
_____
_____
_____

- What are some methods to measure your heart resting rate?

_____
_____
_____
_____
_____
_____
_____
_____
_____

- Explain the process of manually determining your heart rate in bpm.

_____
_____
_____
_____
_____
_____
_____
_____

- What is the normal range for resting heart rate according to the Mayo Clinic?

- How does a lower resting heart rate relate to better cardiovascular fitness?

- What are some factors that can influence your resting heart rate?

_____
_____
_____
_____
_____
_____
_____
_____

- How does body size affect your resting heart rate?

_____
_____
_____
_____
_____
_____
_____
_____
_____

CHAPTER 9

Training: The Minimum Effective Dose to Achieve the Maximum Result

Objectives

- To help acknowledge that exercise is not just for health benefits, but also a baseline requirement for overall wellness and longevity.
- To unveil that exercise is a first-line therapy for treating various diseases and can help improve overall health.
- To prioritize muscle training as a vital component of daily living and recognize its role in protecting our bodies.

Summary

Exercise can be categorized into endurance and strength training, but these distinctions are oversimplified. Resistance exercise training (RET) aims to increase muscle mass and strength through high-tension muscle contractions. Endurance exercise involves low-tension contractions that improve cardiovascular function. High-Intensity Interval Training (HIIT) combines high-intensity bursts with recovery periods. Different training phases target specific adaptations, from stabilization to muscular power.

Exercise starts in the brain, with the mind-muscle connection being crucial. Focusing on the target muscle during exercise can enhance muscle improvement. Directed attention increases activation and reduces contribution from other muscles. Consistent focus improves both mental and physical training outcomes. Setting small, tangible goals and staying consistent are essential.

Some power hacks that can help you achieve your goals include:

1. You can't out-train a bad diet.
2. Complete workouts at least six hours before bedtime.
3. Prioritize the most important exercise in your program first.
4. Recovery is vital, so listen to your body and reframe your perspective on exercise.

Alongside the power hacks, there are about five fundamental attributes that will help achieve fitness goals they are:

1. Courage, which helps you embrace change and overcome limiting beliefs.

2. Perseverance, which allows you to pursue your goals despite difficulties.
3. Self-discipline, which involves resisting temptations and taking steps for your health.
4. Adaptability, to adjust plans when life gets unpredictable.
5. Resilience is the ability to bounce back after setbacks by cultivating emotional intelligence.

Critical lessons from the chapter

- Exercise is the body's strength, and it is an essential component of maintaining health and protecting longevity.

- Never overlook the beauty and power of challenging the body through daily exercises and physical tasks.

- Superior locomotion was crucial for survival in human history and our bodies are designed for physical movement.

- Exercise is a first-line therapy for treating various diseases and can help improve overall health if done accurately.

- Seeing the muscle as medicine and incorporating a well-designed training program.

- Muscle training is a vital element of basic daily living and can act as body armor to protect you.

- Just sitting on the couch while eating protein will not stimulate muscle growth.

Exercises drawn from the chapter

- What are the main categories of exercise mentioned?

_____
_____
_____
_____
_____
_____
_____
_____
_____
_____
_____
_____

- How does Resistance Exercise Training differ from endurance exercise?

- What is the goal of endurance exercise, and how can it be achieved?

- Explain the concept of High-Intensity Interval Training.

_____
_____
_____
_____
_____
_____
_____
_____
_____
_____

- What are the five (5) phases of training according to the National Academy of Sports Medicine?

_____
_____
_____
_____
_____
_____
_____
_____
_____
_____

- How does the mind-muscle connection affect exercise performance?

- What are the key factors in achieving success in fitness goals?

- What does the "You can't out-train a bad diet" power hack mean?

_____
_____
_____
_____
_____
_____
_____
_____
_____
_____

- Why is it recommended to complete workouts at least six hours before bedtime?

_____
_____
_____
_____
_____
_____
_____
_____

- What are the five fundamental attributes discussed for achieving fitness goals, and how do they contribute to success?

CHAPTER 10

Now, You Take the Reins

Objectives

- It aims to help give directions on appropriate training setup and implementation.
- To enable you to make maximum use of the environment around you to keep you on track and on the go.

Summary

Understanding the connection between your personal relationship with external stimuli and your ability to motivate yourself is crucial in achieving long-term health and fitness goals. By shaping your environment with triggers that encourage positive behaviors and discourage negative ones, you can build lasting habits that promote excellence. This can be achieved through strategies like visual reminders of your goals, placing your workout gear strategically, and removing unhealthy temptations. People have different preferences when it comes to workout environments, and these preferences can greatly impact their motivation, from those who thrive in group settings to those who are internally driven. Muscle-centric medicine emphasizes the significance of muscle health in achieving exceptional health and longevity.

To achieve your fitness goals, understanding the role of external factors in motivating yourself is crucial. Shaping your environment with positive triggers and removing negatives is key.

Different workout environments appeal to different people, from group settings to solo workouts. Harnessing these cues in your environment can reinforce your commitment to your fitness journey.

Muscle-Centric Medicine emphasizes the importance of muscle health in promoting longevity and overall well-being. Understanding the significance of muscle in your health can guide your fitness journey.

In maintaining consistent fitness and healthy eating habits, motivation is not enough. Developing a strong self-identity is more reliable for overcoming obstacles and achieving long-term success.

Critical lessons from the chapter

- Visual reminders like posts can be used to inspire mental toughness and act as reminders of the end goal.

- To keep things new and fresh it's advisable to mix up your training environments to also prevent boredom.

- Find a means of connecting with people in the health and wellness space who share your goals and values.

- The Chameleon attribute can help one to adapt and perform well in any environment, whether alone or with others.

- The Solo Act people are internally motivated and don't need external stimuli. Training is normally meditative and therapeutic for them.

- Determining if you thrive in a team setting or prefer to train alone will be very effective in keeping you on track.

- Always find and make use of a place that encourages you to give maximum effort for maximum results.

Exercises drawn from the chapter

- Why is understanding your relationship with external influences important for fitness motivation?

_____
_____
_____
_____
_____
_____
_____
_____

- What strategies can be used to shape your environment for healthier habits?

_____
_____
_____
_____
_____
_____
_____
_____

- How do workout environments influence motivation, and what are the different categories of people in this context?

_____
_____
_____
_____
_____
_____
_____
_____

- What is the central concept of Muscle-Centric Medicine, and how does it relate to health and longevity?

_____
_____
_____
_____
_____
_____
_____
_____

- Why is motivation considered an unreliable factor for consistent fitness and dietary habits?

- What is the significance of muscle health in the context of overall well-being?

- How can visual reminders and quotes contribute to maintaining a healthy lifestyle?

- How can different workout environments impact an individual's motivation and performance?

- What is the role of identity in maintaining consistent fitness habits?

- What are some practical steps for creating a supportive environment for your fitness journey?

Made in United States
Cleveland, OH
21 August 2025